THE
EDWARD

PETER BRIMACOMBE

A PRINCE IN WAITING

The young Albert Edward had a poor relationship with his parents – 'Bertie's propensity is indescribable laziness,' fumed Prince Albert, while Queen Victoria considered her eldest son to be stupid, weak and unfit to rule. As Edward grew up he developed a fascination for beautiful women. His father discovered that Edward had slept with an actress called Nellie Clifden, 'a London lady much run after by the Household Brigade', according to Edward's lifelong friend Charles Carrington. Albert took Edward on a long walk in order to chastise him. It rained heavily; Albert, who had already caught a cold while on a military inspection, developed a chill and died soon afterwards. Although the cause of her beloved husband's premature death was ultimately typhoid, the queen blamed Edward, never forgave him and declared that she could not look at him without a shudder. Only when Edward himself contracted a near fatal disease was a partial reconciliation achieved.

Excluded from any meaningful role in the affairs of state, Edward embarked on a life of pleasure with a string of high-profile mistresses including Lillie Langtry, Alice Keppel and the highly indiscreet Daisy Brooke, 'the babbling Brooke', who later became Countess of Warwick. Edward's affairs were so blatant that he shocked, but at the same time titillated and intrigued, a society only slowly shaking off straight-laced Victorian attitudes –

ABOVE
Young Albert Edward was a difficult child, constantly rude to his teachers and royal servants. As he grew up, both his parents despaired of him ever achieving the high ideals they had set for him.

ABOVE
Queen Victoria and Prince Albert pictured walking in Windsor Great Park at the time of their marriage. When their eldest son Albert Edward was born in 1841 they proved to be unsympathetic parents, lacking in affection towards him.

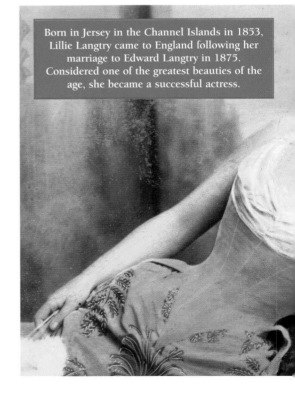

Born in Jersey in the Channel Islands in 1853, Lillie Langtry came to England following her marriage to Edward Langtry in 1875. Considered one of the greatest beauties of the age, she became a successful actress.

ABOVE
HRH Albert Edward, Prince of Wales, and HRH Alexandra,
Princess of Denmark, later King Edward VII and Queen Alexandra.
Seated in an open carriage, they are watched by a massive crowd
as they pass London's St Paul's Cathedral on their wedding day.

he was nicknamed 'Edward the Caresser'. Meanwhile, his mistresses
became popular celebrities – when Lillie Langtry went riding in Hyde
Park, she was applauded by enthusiastic onlookers. Alice Keppel's advice
to a new young royal mistress was 'curtsy first – then jump into bed'.

When Edward married pretty, sweet-natured Princess Alexandra
of Denmark in 1863, Victoria hoped her wayward son might mend his
ways. She was sadly mistaken – the playboy prince continued openly
to wine and dine attractive women at the Ritz or the Café Royal, and
escort them to weekend house parties. Alexandra tolerated Edward's
constant love affairs, even when he was cited in a divorce action –
surprisingly, it proved to be a successful marriage. Together they
established an alternative Court at their London home, Marlborough
House, for those bored by the stilted and gloomy Royal Court, where
Victoria still wore black, even for her Jubilee parade.

Edward had a hearty appetite and ate five large meals a day,
sometimes with ten or more courses. By the time he reached middle
age he was severely overweight – a portly prince in waiting.

A King at Last

When Queen Victoria finally died in January 1901, Edward was nearly 60 years old. After a dissolute life of gambling, horse racing and gorgeous girls, he proved a remarkably popular and successful king, affable and accessible, whereas Victoria had been aloof and unapproachable; highly visible among his citizens, while the queen had been distant and remote.

Edward had travelled widely, visiting France, Italy, India, Egypt and Russia. He was the first British royal to visit the United States of America, where he proved to be extremely popular. This time spent abroad led Edward to develop a passionate interest in foreign affairs. He is credited with playing a significant part in establishing the *Entente Cordiale*, an important treaty with France – traditionally one of Britain's greatest enemies. A new potential foe had emerged – Germany, led by Kaiser Wilhelm, who was thoroughly disliked by the new king, even though he was Wilhelm's uncle. Edward's elder sister Victoria was married to Frederick III, the German emperor, and Wilhelm, their son, succeeded as emperor in 1888.

ABOVE
King Edward VII after his coronation at Westminster Abbey on 9 August 1902. The event was delayed owing to a serious illness.

LEFT
Queen Alexandra, pictured here in 1902, proved to be a popular and supportive queen. She was passionately interested in photography, becoming very proficient as it grew increasingly popular as a hobby in Edwardian England.

ABOVE
Edward and Alexandra transported by elephants during a visit to India. The animals, painted in elaborate designs, their velvet trappings heavily embroidered in gold, encapsulate the splendour of the British Raj in the early 20th century.

the common touch, with a remarkable ability to put people quickly at their ease. Edward was always immaculately dressed; he skilfully modified stiff Victorian outfits, to be more comfortable and practical without sacrificing smartness. Although he had a gargantuan appetite, he drank relatively little yet smoked at least twelve large cigars a day, a habit he inherited from his father, Prince Albert.

Ironically for someone with such a profound interest in the opposite sex, enjoying their wit and intelligence as well as their beauty, Edward opposed women's emancipation, being wholly unsympathetic towards the suffragettes and their campaign for the right to vote in parliamentary elections.

ABOVE
King Edward enthusiastically greets a foreign dignitary during a visit of the ships of the French Navy to Portsmouth in 1905, a colourful example of the newly established *Entente Cordiale*.

Edward was greatly aided in his endeavours by being fluent in both French and German, enabling him to deliver excellent speeches in those countries and thereby endearing himself to their citizens. Indeed, so prominent did he become on the Continent that he was affectionately known as the 'Uncle of Europe'. Edward was the first English monarch to visit Rome and have an audience with the Pope, a gesture that proved very beneficial to Edwardian Roman Catholics.

Edward was short, rather stout and balding, with a distinctive beard and a surprisingly guttural voice. Usually genial and relaxed, he could at times become short-tempered. Nevertheless, he possessed

A King at Last

The king could be equally conservative on other issues, disliking, for example, the introduction of khaki uniforms for the British army. During the First Boer War, British troops, standing upright and clad in scarlet as they had been at the Battle of Waterloo, presented an easy target to the Boers, who wore clothing that blended with the background and unsportingly fired lying down behind trees and other suitable cover. Therefore, when the Second Boer War was fought during Edward's reign, his soldiers wore khaki battledress for the first time. It was during this conflict that Robert Baden-Powell, later founder of the Boy Scout movement, achieved fame at the Siege of Mafeking; and a young Winston Churchill sprang to prominence, when as a war reporter he was captured by the Boers, and then made a daring escape. Rudyard Kipling was also a war correspondent in South Africa at the time.

One of Edward's first actions after becoming king was to give Osborne House, Victoria's favourite home on the Isle of Wight, to the nation. It had unhappy childhood memories. Shortly before he married Alexandra, Edward had purchased the Sandringham estate and built the house that stands today. Edward always celebrated his birthday at Sandringham and began the royal custom of spending Christmas there. Among the many

ABOVE
The Drawing Room at Osborne House on the Isle of Wight.
The house and grounds have recently been extensively restored
and refurbished by English Heritage.

ABOVE
A 1906 portrait of Alice Keppel, who had thick chestnut hair and piercing blue eyes. During the 50th birthday celebrations of the present Prince of Wales, Camilla Parker-Bowles wore jewels bequeathed by Alice Keppel, her great-grandmother.

interesting objects to be seen at Sandringham are the flags that Queen Alexandra gave to the intrepid British explorers Scott and Shackleton for their expeditions to the South Pole.

Edward was on the throne for less than a decade yet, like his mother before him, gave his name to an era. He reshaped the monarchy into an institution relevant to a modern democracy and pioneered the constitutional role of a contemporary Head of State, a remarkable achievement in view of his lack of training for the role and Victoria's constant dread that he would take the nation back to the dissipated days of the Regency period. Yet Edward had learned much by observation and experience, displaying an instinctive grasp of the appropriate role for a monarch in a rapidly changing world. While his achievements as king have been overshadowed by his colourful life as Prince of Wales, arguably Edward VII remains one of the nation's most underrated monarchs.

As he lay dying at Buckingham Palace in May 1910, both his wife Queen Alexandra and his long-term mistress, Alice Keppel, were at his bedside. The new king, Edward's son who became George V, wrote in his diary, 'At 11.45 beloved Papa passed peacefully away and I have lost my best friend and the best of fathers.'

HIGH SOCIETY

When Edward ascended the throne following Victoria's death, Lord Salisbury was Prime Minister, it being perfectly normal at that time for the nation's affairs to be directed from the House of Lords. Yet the political landscape was beginning to change; in 1892 Keir Hardie had been elected as the first Labour MP, causing a stir by arriving at the House of Commons wearing a cloth cap and accompanied by a brass band. A radical young Welshman named David Lloyd George was beginning to make his mark with a series of fiery speeches. The equally able orator Winston Churchill, who had first been elected to parliament in 1900, was appointed a cabinet minister in Asquith's government at the age of 34, eight years later. Meanwhile the nation resounded to the strident voices of the suffragettes.

Edwardian society was also undergoing a subtle change as new money from successful business and finance mixed with the old money of a landed aristocracy highly adept at overcoming a financial crisis by marrying into money. These newcomers to

ABOVE
A photograph *c*.1904 of the Welsh Liberal, David Lloyd George, who later became Prime Minister and, in the spirit of the times, reputedly kept a mistress in Downing Street.

BELOW
An elegant crowd gathers for church on a Sunday in June 1907. Spearheaded by the Oxford Movement, religion enjoyed a huge revival in the late 19th century, when many new churches were created.

ABOVE
A young Winston Churchill attentively awaits game birds during a pheasant shoot in December 1910. Six years earlier, Churchill had abandoned the Tories and crossed the floor of the House of Commons to join the Liberals.

wealth and privilege were joined by an entirely new phenomenon, the press baron. Alfred Harmsworth, soon to become Lord Northcliffe, astutely realized that newspaper readers liked to be entertained as well as informed, and he introduced the popular press, full of sport, fashion and gossip. Northcliffe launched the *Daily Mail* in 1896, followed by the *Daily Mirror* in 1903. He also purchased both *The Times* and *The Observer*. A megalomaniac with delusions of grandeur, Northcliffe wielded colossal power through his newspapers, even having the ability to bring down governments – or so he thought. Certainly he invented mass-circulation tabloid journalism.

The focal point for Edwardian political movers and social shakers was the weekend party held at great country houses such as Chatsworth, Blenheim and Polesden Lacey. These were the powerhouses where affairs of state and business were settled in a relaxed world of authority and affluence populated by princes, prime ministers and other major players in Edwardian society. Winston Churchill had been born unexpectedly while his parents, Lord and Lady Randolph Churchill, were attending a party at Blenheim. 'Although present at that occasion, I have no recollection of the events leading up to it,' Churchill later quipped.

Edward moved easily within this sparkling scene, and society took its cue from the impeccably attired king – a primary reason for the Edwardian era being such a gracious age, full of elegant ladies and immaculately dressed gentlemen.

ABOVE
An idealistic, almost evangelical, 1910 advertisement promotes women's rights as part of the sustained suffragette campaign to enable women to vote in parliamentary elections.

THE SUFFRAGETTES

This term was one of derision invented by a *Daily Mail* reporter. Its most prominent figure was Emmeline Pankhurst, deceptively ladylike in appearance with 'the face of a weary saint', yet gleefully admitting 'I love fighting'.

After years of violent demonstrations and hunger strikes in Holloway Prison, the House of Lords finally passed a bill giving all adult women the right to vote in 1928, the year Emmeline Pankhurst died.

A LEISURELY LIFE ON THE OCEAN WAVE

At the dawn of the 20th century, Britain possessed the world's largest and most powerful navy, whose authority had not been challenged since Trafalgar nearly a century earlier. Hardly a shot had been fired in anger for many years; indeed, gunnery was positively discouraged as it dirtied well-scrubbed decks. Naval officers were more experienced at cocktail parties than combat, their well-tanned faces and crisp white tropical uniforms causing many a female heart to flutter. The Edwardian navy had become the finest yacht club in the world, as it cruised to foreign exotic ports for a seemingly endless round of parties, pretty girls and polo, while showing the flag to impress the natives during this high tide of British imperialism.

ABOVE
HMS *Dreadnought* leading a line of battleships in 1906, the year this mighty warship was launched – a time when Britain truly ruled the waves, with powerful fleets in every part of the world.

ABOVE
Edward VII photographed *c*.1903 in an open carriage with his nephew Kaiser Wilhelm II. They sport near-identical plumed hats, as befits an auspicious ceremonial occasion.

Occasionally it became necessary to send a gunboat to quell some misguided insurgent. During one such foray up the River Nile, the dashing young naval officer David Beatty met an equally dashing young Hussar named Winston Churchill. Beatty apparently introduced Churchill to champagne. Beatty became an admiral and Commander of the Fleet, while Churchill took part in the British army's last cavalry charge during the Battle of Omdurman in 1898. These, however, were minor skirmishes on the frontier of empire, a glorious game with little risk to life or limb. The greatest danger for the unwary young officer was to be ensnared by 'the fishing fleet', a group of predatory young women in search of husbands.

The duties of a young officer ranged from entertaining visiting dignitaries, with pink gins in the wardroom, to attending a grand ball in honour of royalty. At one such glittering event staged in Plymouth in 1891 for Edward's younger brother, Alfred, HRH The Duke of Edinburgh, more than 1,000 guests consumed 576 bottles of champagne, 540 bottles of spirits and 6,800 oysters.

These were indeed halcyon days but storm clouds were gathering on the horizon. Across the North Sea, Edward's despised nephew Kaiser Wilhelm was building a mighty German fleet to rival the Royal Navy. In 1906 Britain launched HMS *Dreadnought*, the world's first all big-gun battleship; fast and heavily armed, making all existing battleships seem obsolete, it appeared to guarantee continuing British superiority. This belief was to be rudely shattered at the Battle of Jutland – yet this was some considerable time ahead. Meanwhile, it was still blue skies, sparkling seas – and definitely time for another pink gin.

THE SEASON

Edward leads his horse Persimmon into the Winners' Enclosure after he had won the 1896 Derby. As king he won the Derby on two further occasions, a feat not achieved by any other British monarch.

The Edwardians loved to enjoy themselves and be entertained. Affluent Edwardian society did the season, a hectic round of glamorous even at Epsom, Ascot, Lords, Henley, Cowes and Wimbledon, interspersed with glittering balls, sumptuous banquets and shooting parties. The cream of society was on parade dressed in all their finery – th to see and be seen. Everywhere amid this frenetic soci whirl eager young ladies energetically pursued eligible young men in search of a suitable husband, preferably with wealth and a title.

At the epicentre of this colourful throng was the familiar bearded figure of Edward, a keen and capable participant. Having created the Royal Stud at Sandringham, his horse Persimmon won both the Der and the St Leger in 1896, then the Ascot Gold Cup th following year. An enthusiastic and skilful sailor of the royal yacht *Britannia*, Edward invariably attended Cow Week, organized by that most exclusive club, the Roya Yacht Squadron, where class rather than cash was the key to entry. His success ended when Kaiser Wilhelm appeared with a larger, faster yacht; Edward retired in a huff and never raced again. Edward's enthusiasm and continual presence did much to boost the kudos of th season. Queen Victoria shunned such frivolity and preferred to remain in isolation at Windsor, Osborne or even further afield at Balmoral.

John Strickland Goodall's colourful painting of Cowes Regatta, an important event in the Edwardian season for both competitor and spectator. Many of the latter may well have spent more time watching each other instead of the yachts in the Solent.

Those less privileged flocked to sporting events, the theatre and the music hall. Theatre-goers could choose between the witty sophistication of Oscar Wilde, George Bernard Shaw's cerebral comedies or the cheerful easy listening provided by the operettas of Gilbert and Sullivan. This pair had an uneasy relationship; Gilbert was bombastic and temperamental, the frustrated Sullivan wished to be recognized as a classical composer but was singularly unsuccessful. The impresario Richard d'Oyly Carte attempted to keep the peace, yet the quarrelsome partnership once worked together for an entire year without speaking. Nevertheless they produced hugely popular work such as *The Mikado* and *HMS Pinafore*. More serious music was provided by Delius and Vaughan Williams, together with Edward Elgar, who was much admired by King Edward. Equally popular was the Edwardian music hall, featuring a colourful cast of comedians, singers, dancers, acrobats and jugglers including Marie Lloyd, Harry Lauder, Vesta Tilley and a very young Charlie Chaplin, who first appeared on the stage aged five. All performed under the urbane direction of the ubiquitous Master of Ceremonies, 'introducing your very, very own …'.

ABOVE
A portrait of the eminent English composer Edward Elgar, set against the uncompleted Royal Albert Hall. Elgar and the architect Edwin Lutyens epitomized English culture during the Edwardian era.

ROYAL COMMAND PERFORMANCE

King Edward requested that lyrics be added to the music of Elgar's *Pomp and Circumstance, March No 1*. A.C. Benson wrote these in 1902, resulting in *Land of Hope and Glory*, now a popular feature at the Last Night of the Proms, initiated by Henry Wood at the Royal Albert Hall in 1895.

BELOW
An art nouveau postcard depicting *The Mikado*, one of Gilbert and Sullivan's most successful operettas, complete with geisha girls and oriental lanterns. Gilbert and Sullivan's work remained popular throughout Edward's reign.

THE EDWARDIAN HOUSE PARTY

An essential ingredient in Edwardian society's lavish lifestyle was the weekend party, where gentlemen could slaughter exceedingly large quantities of pheasants while the ladies exchanged the latest gossip, showed off extravagant outfits and joined the men for elaborate picnics. Guests would consume vast quantities of food and drink, flirt outrageously over the dinner table, play cards or billiards – and perhaps indulge in late-night amorous assignations.

This hedonism would take place either in great aristocratic stately homes or the opulent houses of nouveau riche, intensely ambitious social climbers using their newly acquired wealth to secure a place in high society. Typical of the latter was Mrs Ronald Grenville, whose father had made a fortune in the Scottish brewing industry. His upwardly mobile daughter had married the Honourable Ronald Grenville, a dashing captain in the Life Guards and close friend of Alice Keppel's husband George. This astute move gave her instant access into the king's elite Marlborough House set. Mrs Grenville then acquired Polesden Lacey, an attractive Regency house in Surrey, which was considerably enlarged to provide a suitable stage for her legendary weekend parties; here, Indian maharajas mingled with British cabinet ministers and the cream of European royalty, including Kaiser Wilhelm, Grand Duke Michael of Russia and, of course, King Edward, a frequent guest at Polesden Lacey.

ABOVE
Numerous guests were entertained at Lanhydrock, Cornwall, during the Edwardian period – the cook could be assisted by up to a dozen servants. The kitchen's high gabled roof and mullioned windows resemble a college hall.

RIGHT
The Edwardian aristocrat Lord Ribblesdale, painted by John Singer Sargent, the favourite society portrait painter of the day. The aristocracy's luxurious lifestyle was targeted with punitive new taxes by the radical social reformer David Lloyd George.

The main living areas of the Edwardian country house were divided into spheres of male and female influence. The drawing room and boudoir were ladies' territory; the library, billiards room and smoking room represented an all-male preserve, where men gathered to smoke, drink brandy and indulge in conversation considered inappropriate for female ears. The dining room was common ground, where a constant procession of elaborate meals would follow each other with clockwork precision.

Guests were pampered by an army of servants who were inexpensive and readily available, and who considered it a privilege to serve. They, too, lived in a strictly segregated world, male servants ruled by the all-powerful butler, females by a matriarchal housekeeper. While outwardly deferential, servants could be more snobbish than those they served, closely scrutinizing the clothes and luggage of newly arriving guests to assess the potential size of their tips!

Thus the outwardly carefree weekend party presented the hostess with a challenge requiring the organizational expertise of a military commander, and at the same time representing a social commando course for her guests who needed both skill and stamina in order to survive.

ABOVE
The queen's head carving by Edward Lutyens at Hestercombe in Somerset. The garden was created between 1904 and 1909 by Lutyens and Gertrude Jekyll.

EDWARDIAN GARDENERS

Edwin Lutyens and Gertrude Jekyll were an unlikely combination. The matronly spinster was twice the age of the aspiring young architect when they met, yet their partnership lasted more than 40 years. They created definitive Edwardian gardens where Lutyens provided the paths, pools, walls, terraces, seats and pergolas for Jekyll's exuberant planting. Arguably, Hestercome in Somerset represents the best of their work still accessible to the public.

ABOVE
Chatsworth in Derbyshire, the seat of the Dukes of Devonshire. The 8th Duke and his wife Louise entertained lavishly at Chatsworth, mainly in the autumn and winter. King Edward and Queen Alexandra were regular visitors.

LEFT
A 1911 house party gathering for a shoot at Stonor Park near Henley-on-Thames, Oxfordshire, home of Lord and Lady Camoys, whose family has owned the property for more than 800 years.

LITERARY LONDON

The nation's literary tradition continued strongly into the Edwardian epoch and many great writers emanated from this period, among them George Bernard Shaw, Rudyard Kipling, Sir Arthur Conan Doyle, J.M. Barrie and James Priestley, who later wrote *The Edwardians*, an absorbing book based on personal memories of events and leading figures of the day. Shaw's play *Pygmalion* was subsequently destined to achieve international acclaim as the stage and film musical *My Fair Lady*. Conan Doyle invented the famous fictional detective Sherlock Holmes, while J.M. Barrie created that appealing children's fantasy *Peter Pan*.

Literary London revolved around Bloomsbury, where a cosmopolitan collection of writers, artists and intellectuals known as the Bloomsbury Set led a bohemian lifestyle, 'living in squares and loving in triangles', as an observer wittily noted. The group included Lytton Strachey, an iconoclastic writer, the American-born T.S. Eliot, perhaps the most gifted poet of his generation, and E.M. Forster, whose brilliant collection of novels included *A Room with a View* and *Howard's End*. The Bloomsbury Set had been founded by the novelist Virginia Woolf and her artist sister Vanessa Bell at 46 Gordon Square. The group's unconventional behaviour and constantly

Theatre-goers in full evening dress leave His Majesty's Theatre in London's Haymarket during 1907. Attending the theatre in the Edwardian age was invariably a glamorous occasion.

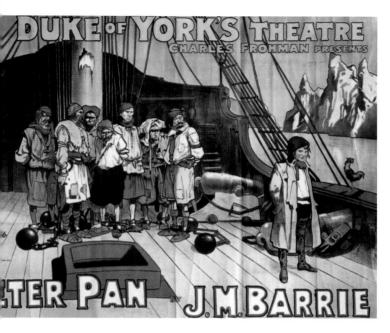

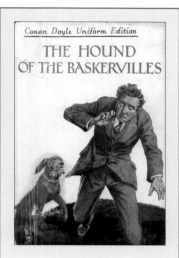

nterchanging relationships kept Edwardian tongues wagging at a furious rate, particularly when Vanessa set up a *ménage à trois* with her husband Clive and fellow artist Duncan Grant – a relationship that was to last several decades.

The Bloomsbury Set's antics paled into insignificance compared with the sensational trial and subsequent imprisonment of Oscar Wilde in 1895, having been found guilty of homosexual offences. Wilde's dazzling career came to an abrupt halt. When released from Reading Gaol two years later, he went to live in Paris and never returned to London, where he had been the darling of an English society enthralled by his sparkling prose and glamorous lifestyle.

The Bloomsbury Set's carefree London existence ended when Vanessa Bell, together with husband and lover, moved permanently from their town house to Charleston, an idyllic farmhouse in the lee of the South Downs in Sussex. At the same time Virginia Woolf and her literary husband Leonard went to the nearby village of Rodmell. The tortured Virginia later committed suicide by drowning herself in the nearby River Ouse.

Great artistry usually reflects the mood of a nation during a particular period of time. Wilde's ultra-sophisticated wit and Forster's perceptive insight come closest to capturing the essence of Edwardian England.

THE MAN WHO INVENTED SHERLOCK HOLMES

Sir Arthur Conan Doyle was born in Edinburgh in 1859. Having qualified as a doctor, he worked as a senior physician in a field hospital during the Second Boer War. He wrote his famous thriller *The Hound of the Baskervilles* in 1902 while staying in a hotel on Dartmoor, having been inspired by local legend. In later years he became a spiritualist.

A DECADE OF PROGRESS

Much has been made of the frivolity of the Edwardian age, yet this was a time when the march of technology almost broke into a gallop, a period that saw the development of the motor car, the aeroplane, radio communications and the cinema.

In 1904, Charles Rolls met Henry Royce, and two years later the first Rolls Royce was constructed – the Silver Ghost, considered to be the epitome of luxury and style in the Edwardian era. When the 'horseless carriage' had first appeared, it was legally required to travel at a speed of less than four miles per hour, preceded by a man with a red flag. When this ludicrously restrictive law was abolished in 1896, motorists celebrated with a run from London to Brighton, an event that still takes place every autumn when several hundred veteran cars set out from London's Hyde Park in the direction of the seafront at Brighton. King Edward became the first British monarch to own a motor car, a Daimler Phaeton purchased in 1900. Today it can be seen at Sandringham, still in full working order. This increasingly popular form of transport meant that the horse-drawn hansom cab was rapidly replaced by a motorized version, and motor racing commenced at Brooklands in 1907.

The first successful aeroplane flight in England took place in 1908. Two years later, Charles Rolls, as keen on aeroplanes as motor cars, flew both ways non stop across the English Channel, only to be killed in an aeroplane crash shortly afterwards.

ABOVE
A 1905 20-horsepower Rolls Royce, runner up in the Tourist Trophy Race that year. Sitting behind the driver is Charles Stewart Rolls, who founded the company with Henry Royce the previous year.

BELOW
The *Daily Mail* offered a £10,000 prize for the first aviator to fly between London and Manchester in less than 24 hours. The Frenchman Louis Paulhan succeeded in a Farman biplane in April 1910.

In 1901, the Italian Guglielmo Marconi successfully established radio contact from North Cornwall across the Atlantic Ocean to Newfoundland. Marconi's invention revolutionized international communications and he was awarded the Nobel Prize for Physics in 1909. Ernest Rutherford pioneered atomic science in a laboratory at Cambridge University; he, too, won a Nobel Prize, in 1908.

The first English cinema opened in London the same year. Among the early film stars were the English-born Charlie Chaplin and Stan Laurel. The latter established a partnership with Oliver Hardy that became one of the most successful comedy acts in cinema history. Sadly, in years to come, the growing popularity of the cinema led to the demise of the music hall.

Thus in the short span of Edward's reign, not even a decade, the nation experienced massive technological progress, which was to be of great benefit for generations to come.

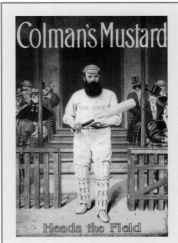

ABOVE
W.G. Grace features on a Colman's Mustard advertisement, an early example of a prominent sportsman being used to promote a commercial product.

DEFINITELY NOT OUT!

W.G. Grace is one of the most enduring figures of English cricket. Immensely talented, he scored 54,896 runs and took nearly 3,000 wickets in first-class games. He played on 22 occasions for England. Flawless technique was accompanied by autocratic behaviour; when a lesser-known player clean-bowled him, Grace replaced the bails and prepared to play on. 'They have come to watch me bat, not you bowl,' he snapped.

ABOVE
The Italian physicist and inventor Marconi, with an assistant standing at his side, at work in his laboratory c.1903. Aged only 29 at the time, he had already successfully sent the first radio message across the Atlantic from England.

LEFT
A poster for a London cinema – surprisingly there were films available in colour in 1911! The earliest colour film – kinemacolor – had been patented in Britain by George Albert Smith five years earlier.

LENGTHENING SHADOWS

Edwardian England was a green and pleasant land for those with plenty of money, although the more perceptive had an uneasy feeling that it could not last for ever. 'We are living in difficult times,' declared the king, sensing that the world was marching relentlessly to war as great armies gathered throughout Continental Europe. At home the nation faced a constitutional crisis as the Liberal-controlled House of Commons continually clashed with a Tory-dominated House of Lords and much of the working class population lived in poverty. Edward was not destined to see the outcome of these crucial issues. The good life finally caught up with him and he died in 1910 aged 69 after a series of heart attacks.

Crowds pay their respects to King Edward as he lies in state at Westminster Hall in London after his death in early May 1910. Queen Alexandra, who was three years younger than the king, lived until 1925.